Misery Bear's
Guide to Love
& heartbreak

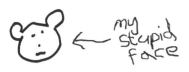
my stupid face

contents

wish i could smile

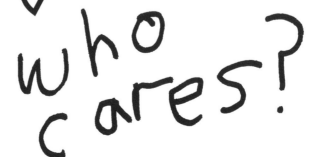
who cares?

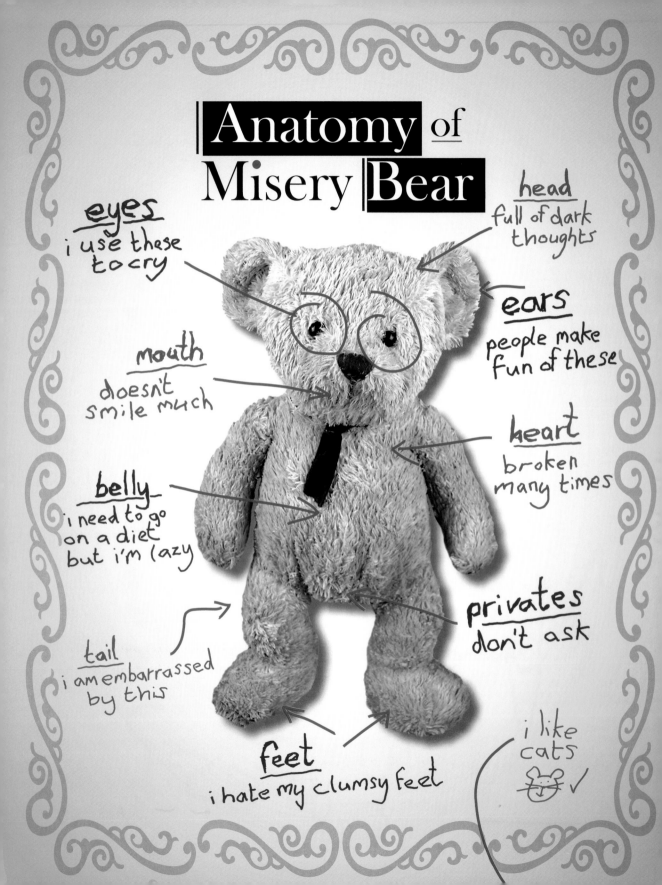

Hello

My name is Misery Bear. I know, it's a pretty horrible name, isn't it? I wish I'd been called something nice like Trevor or Mr Fluffington, but there you go. That's life.

So this is my guide to love and romance, but mainly heartbreak, which I've got lots of experience of. I do my best to impress the ladies, but for some reason my furry little heart gets mushed up over and over again. Don't worry, the drink gets me through it. Just.

Thank you for buying my book. I'll try not to let you down. Although I usually do...

misery
bear
xx

depression - bear... ⊗ | snowboarding - go... ⊗ | Shattered Hearts ⊗ | helicopters ⊗

My Profile | Inbox (0) | Matches (0) | Viewed (0) | Winks (0)

Last logged in: **Online Now!**

M_BEAR01

I am VERY lonely and VERY available

Status: single
Height: 1' 2"
Body Type: below average
Hair: excessive
Eyes: black
Hometown: London, UK
Looking for: females

Interested in: just friends, long-term relationship, anything

Occupation: not specified

Education: primary, some college

Qualifications: GCSE English, first aid basics certificate, bartender training, unlocked 'Prestige' mode on *Bear of Duty*, one salsa lesson

Smoking: some of the time

Drinking: all of the time

Likes: drinking, smoking, honey, helicopters, drawing, toast, Jessica Alba, cloudy days, car chases, dreaming I'm amazing, whisky, Batman

Dislikes: hangovers, haircuts, running out of mixers, trapping my paws in doors, big bicycles, ghosts

CONGRATULATIONS! YOU HAVE 00 MATCHES

BAD DATES

I met Maria in a bar where she was dancing on a table. She was lots of fun, and she did cartwheels for money. On our date we went dancing in a disco. She was quickly chatted up by a very handsome bear called Jeff.

I got a kebab on my way home and watched *Star Wars* on my own.

I've no idea what she's doing now, although I think I've seen her in a video on the web.

Name: *Maria Mendoza*
Nationality: *Brazilian*
Likes: *dancing*
Dislikes: *dancing with me*

Gina
ality:
very
: not

Romantic Days Out: Picnic

Picnics are a good way to romance a member of whatever sex you want to do things with.

WHY PICNICS ARE GOOD: outdoor drinking, flowers, cupcakes, jam sandwiches, looking at clouds, al fresco canoodling

WHY PICNICS ARE BAD: angry bees, angry ants, angry wasps, hay fever, getting locked in the park, dog plops

Love Letter #1

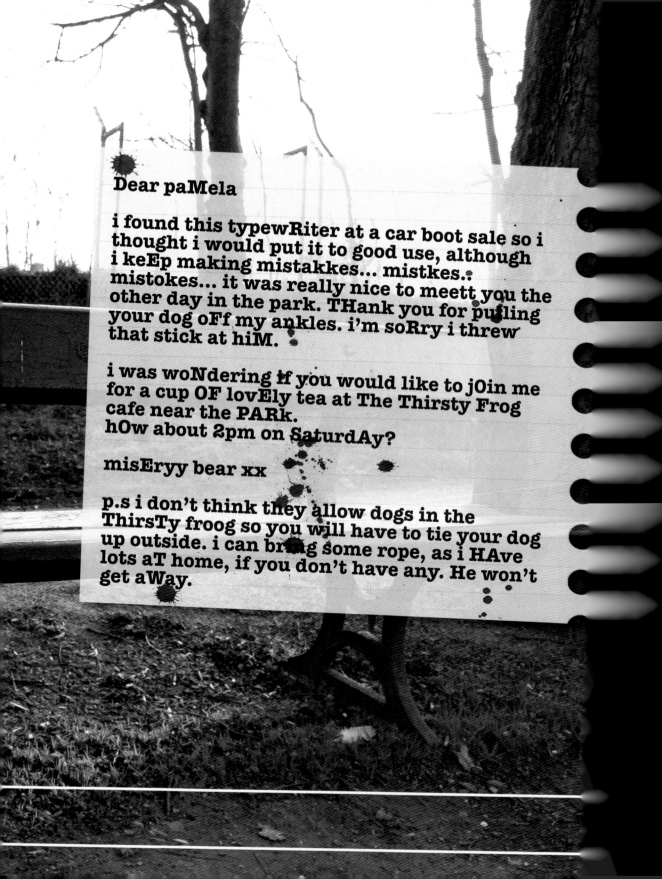

Dear paMela

i found this typewRiter at a car boot sale so i thought i would put it to good use, although i keEp making mistakkes... mistkes... mistokes... it was really nice to meett you the other day in the park. THank you for pulling your dog oFf my ankles. i'm soRry i threw that stick at hiM.

i was woNdering if you would like to jOin me for a cup OF lovEly tea at The Thirsty Frog cafe near the PARk.
hOw about 2pm on SaturdAy?

misEryy bear xx

p.s i don't think they allow dogs in the ThirsTy froog so you will have to tie your dog up outside. i can bring some rope, as i HAve lots aT home, if you don't have any. He won't get aWay.

Dating Tips for the Lonely

The dating game is a minefield, and I should know – I've blown my legs off loads of times. Here's how to keep your heart intact.

MAKE SURE YOU'RE ON TIME

It's OK for women to be a bit late, but men – and bears – should always be on time. I usually get to a venue four hours before my date arrives to get the best table. And to get hammered.

LOOK YOUR BEST

I'll never forget when I turned up to a date wearing a pink hat. It was a bad idea and I shouldn't have taken the advice from the man who sold me the hat.

COMPLIMENT YOUR DATE

Humans love compliments whereas us bears get easily embarrassed. I go bright red and have to go and wash my face in the sink. A good example of a compliment is: 'You smell okay!' Another one is: 'Your ears are pretty.'

DON'T DISCUSS PREVIOUS RELATIONSHIPS

I once dated a girl who constantly talked about how great her ex was. To be honest, he did sound pretty cool. So when he unexpectedly turned up I shook his hand and then watched as he led my date out of the door. Sigh.

AVOID WEIRD TOPICS

Never mention religion, stomach complaints, mice, the 1982 bear riots, operations or aliens. I try not to mention the time I tried to hang myself from a door handle using a belt. Really puts people off their pudding.

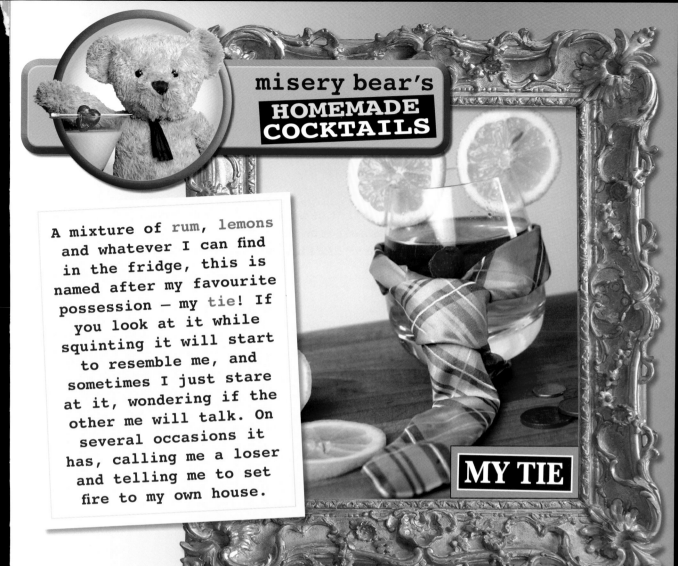

misery bear's HOMEMADE COCKTAILS

A mixture of rum, lemons and whatever I can find in the fridge, this is named after my favourite possession — my tie! If you look at it while squinting it will start to resemble me, and sometimes I just stare at it, wondering if the other me will talk. On several occasions it has, calling me a loser and telling me to set fire to my own house.

MY TIE

a miserable life

THE BEAR WHO LOVED ME → *or "the bear with ;?? the golden gun?.? "live and let bear!*

Scene 20

INT. CASINO. NIGHT

MISERY BEAR walks into the casino in a tuxedo. He looks
really cool and everybody wants to be him.

                    BARTENDER
            May I get you a drink, sir?

make it 18 martinis

                    MISERY BEAR
            Eight martinis. Four shaken, four
                    stirred. Please.

An attractive woman, ANNA MALL, walks up to MISERY BEAR.
She is a spy but he doesn't know it yet.

note: Anna must be gorgeous

                    ANNA
            I don't believe we've had the
                pleasure. I'm Anna Mall.

                    MISERY BEAR
            I'm an animal too. Coincidence?

MISERY BEAR raises his eyebrow. ANNA smiles. She wants to
marry him. MISERY BEAR holds out his hand.

                    MISERY BEAR (CONT'D)
            The name's Bear. Misery Bear.

                    ANNA
            Hmm. Are you pleased to see me or
            is that a gun in your trousers?

                    MISERY BEAR
            It's a gun in my trousers.

M15ery bear?

                    BARTENDER
            That will be £110 pounds please.

                    MISERY BEAR
            What? That's too expensive.

MISERY BEAR and the BARTENDER have a fight. MISERY BEAR is
brilliant and throws the BARTENDER out of the window and
he dies. ANNA really fancies MISERY BEAR now. *They kiss.*

                    ANNA
            Looks like I'll have to keep my eyes
                    on you.

                    MISERY BEAR
            Try taking them off me.

MISERY BEAR suddenly fights some henchmen. ← *this will be cool!!!*

Misery Bear
is

THE BEAR WHO LOVED ME

Bear Facts

Some random facts about bears that you might not have known. None of them are made up.

roar!

Pandas are rubbish in bed.

Don't run from a bear. He's probably trying to give you something.

Alcoholism is a problem in the bear community. As is honeyism.

Human men who call themselves 'bears' on the internet are lying.

Grizzly bears love to be tickled. Try it on the next one you see.

Bears that eat too much honey get sticky sweat.

Koalas aren't bears. I hate koalas. If I ever met a koala I'd punch it on the nose.

Never lend money to a polar bear – you won't see it again.

top 5 songs to drink gin in the bath to

After a long day at the office, I like a good soak to get all the grime and smell of humans off me. With gin.

5

Only Love Can Break Your Heart
by Neil Young

He's a scruffy, whiny man, Neil Young, but he sings the truth. Nothing else can come close to breaking your heart like love can. I've loved a lot but don't recall being loved back. Thanks, life.

4

re: stacks by Bon Iver

Silly name for a song, but it grabs hold of my little furry heart and shakes it about like a hungry wolf with a hen. When I listen to it I get the sniffles.

Hurt by Johnny Cash

I like to think Johnny Cash and I would have made good drinking buddies back in the day. I wear my black tie in honour of him. Not bad for a human.

3

2

Eleanor Rigby
by The Beatles

'Ahhhh, look at all the lonely people.' Some times that lyric sounds sarcastic, and feels like Lennon is laughing at me.

Boys Don't Cry by The Cure

This one totally works if you change the lyrics to 'bears don't cry.' Of course, we do cry but I think the man in The Cure who wears the lipstick was being ironic when he wrote it.

1

As Cold as My Heart

The winter cold
Makes me shiver
You look at me
And make me quiver

We go to yours
For some dinner
You serve me up
A plate of liver

I vomit for eight hours

Celebrity Love List

Some of the lovely ladies I would very much like to go out with please. If you know any of them, please pass on my details...

ANGELINA JOLIE

She scares me a little bit, and I worry she might be a bit rough with little bears like me. I would like to invite Angelina to my place for peanut butter sandwiches and kissing.

KYLIE

I sent Kylie a tweet once asking her on a date. She tweeted me back, 'OK'. True story. So have I been on a date with her? No. Bit rude of her if you ask me.

HALLE BERRY

I saw her in a film once where her top was off. Ever since then, I've had dreams about her where we're married and her top is always off.

misery bear's
HOMEMADE COCKTAILS

This is made using rum, cream, a banana and a couple of paracetamol to help with the hangover the next day. It's a fun drink and will put a sparkle in the eye of anybody you serve it to. Also, it can be made without the banana and I actually prefer it that way. I hate bananas.

BANANA DAQUIRI

a miserable life

Tokyo: Got squished on the subway, couldn't understand anyone. Got v drunk on sake.

Girls met: 0
Godzillas seen: 0

Destination HEART ACHE

Ever since they finally gave me a passport, I've trotted the globe in search of romance. Have I found any? Have I f***

i like holidays!

Amsterdam: Went into a very weird coffee shop and can't remember what happened.

Girls met: (lots, but they were in windows)
Clogs worn: 0

Name: Misery Bear
Address:
City:
State: Zip:
No:

Sydney: 24 hr flight, filled 2 sick bags, refused entry into Sydney Opera House. Chased by a funnel web spider.

Girls met: 0
Kangaroos kicked by: 1

New York: Busy city, got bitten by horse in Central Park, a taxi driver called me an 'asshole'.

Girls met: 1
(Statue of Liberty)

PASSENGER NAME **MISERY BEAR**
FROM: LONDON
TO: NEW YORK
FLIGHT AA116
GROUP 6   GATE 4   BOARD 11
160   472 21

Munich: Oktoberfest, Woke up in hospital getting tummy pumped.

Girls met: 10 (nurses)
Girls kissed: 0 (I got sick in my fur)

My Best Chat-up lines*

Your hair's nice. Can I smell it?

I'm feeling too hairy. Fancy giving me a shave?

You've got an amazing face.

If you were a toad, you'd be the best toad in the pond.

I never like to beg, but will you please, please, please, go out with me?

Excuse me, are you a thief, because you've stolen my heart. I also just saw you shop-lifting.

You make me sick with love. Can you help me wipe it up?

Hey you just trod on my feet! Would you like a drink?

*These have NEVER worked

Romantic Days Out:  Gallery

Galleries are basically big posh houses full of old pictures. Perfect for impressing your date!

WHY GALLERIES ARE GOOD:
no dogs, they make you seem clever, pictures of naked ladies (sometimes)

WHY GALLERIES ARE BAD:
boring, full of weirdos

facebear

Search

Wall
Info
Photos (500)
Info
Friends (15)

 Bashful Bruin

 Lisa H

 Pete Shirley

 Petrie

 Werner Herzog

 Paul Doolan

MiseryBear

♥ Married to No-one 🏠 From London, UK 🗓 Born on 29 February 1980
💼 Work Blurgh 🎓 Education MA in Philosophy

Share: 💬 **Post** 🐻 **Photo** 🔗 **Link** 📹 **Video**

 Misery Bear
Will this pain never end?
9 minutes ago

 Rupert B
Man up.
8 minutes ago

Paddington B
Come round mine later. I've got some DVDs.
6 minutes ago

 Misery Bear
@Rupert, screw you. @Paddington, not after last time.
4 minutes ago

 Misery Bear
Does anyone want to come to the park with me?
1 hour ago

 Gentle Ben
No.
58 minutes ago

 Honk
No.
58 minutes ago

 Yogi
No thanks.
51 minutes ago

 David Attenbear
Piss off.
41 minutes ago

 Bertie Bear
No.
38 minutes ago

(18)

Dear Misery

A problem shared is a problem multiplied. Or is that halved? Subtracted? I can't remember. Whatever, here are my replies to your problems...

Dear Misery Bear
My girlfriend told me she is seeing somebody else and has broken up with me. I'm so upset, and I can't stop thinking about her and the times we spent together. What can I do?
Mike Paptch

Dear Mike
I've been rejected and dumped by lots of people, and the good news is that one day the sun will consume the Earth and we'll all be dead. Until then, do what I do: drink until it doesn't hurt any more. Or at least until you pass out.
MB

Dear Misery Bear
I really fancy the guy who works in my local coffee shop but I'm too shy to say anything. How can I let him know my feelings without making a fool of myself?
Sandra Durks

Dear Sandra
If I were in your situation I would order a coffee and then say 'I love you'. This probably explains why I don't have a girlfriend, so don't do that. Why don't you just ask me out instead? I'm available.
MB

Dear Misery Bear
I sometimes feel very alone, as if I'm not a part of the real world but just isolated all by myself. I walk around like a ghost that nobody sees or cares about.
Mr Pipes

Dear Mr Pipes
I am sorry to hear that you feel alone. You say you feel a bit like a ghost, and reading your letter again I'm starting to wonder if that's what you are. I don't mind, but please don't haunt my home because I would be absolutely terrified.
MB

Dear Misery Bear
My wife thinks you're gorgeous and we were wondering if you would like to come around one evening for some 'fun'. My wife makes a great shepherd's pie and we've also got a snooker table. What do you say?
Phil and Brenda

Dear Phil and Brenda
Okay, that sounds cool. I like shepherd's pie, and while I'm not very good at snooker, it will beat staying in on my own. Ohh... wait a minute... oh, right – 'fun'. No. No, I don't want to come over, you perverts.
MB

Dear Misery Bear
I think the spark has gone out of my marriage. What can I do to put the spark back into it again?
Becky Grinsdale

Dear Becky
Every night I come home from my dead-end job, microwave a meal-for-one, put my paws up in front of the telly and sink half a bottle of bourbon. Some days, I can barely get out of bed, I'm so tired of my awful, worthless life. I cry all the time, and some days go by without a single person talking to me. Get over yourself.
MB

misery bear's HOMEMADE COCKTAILS

This is made with a liqueur that I can't spell, and while it's very tasty it will turn your tongue blue. It's a romantic cocktail because the little umbrella will remind your partner of romantic holidays. It only reminds me of torrential rain. Best served with two cigarettes.

BLUE LAGOON

a miserable life

A Bear's Guide to Grooming

1 WASH EVERYTHING
No one likes a dirty bear so you should wash at least twice a day. I hate washing because it takes me ages to get dry, especially in my intimate areas. Also, I have very sensitive eyes, skin and ears.

2 SPRAY YOURSELF
People like nice smells, so if you're not getting any action there's a good chance you niff like farts. Ladies always smell nice, for some reason. My favourite cologne is 'Musky Sausage - Pour Bear'. Makes me feel tough.

3 THE BEARD RULE
Some women love stubble on a man but remember, guys - women never trust men with beards. I don't either; I think they're really weird. Also, a lot of women don't like to shave their legs and that's fine with me. Although I draw the line at hairy feet. That's just mental.

4 MOUTH TO MOUTH
If I've been spending the whole day drinking, smoking and eating spicy Thai peanuts, there's a good chance my mouth smells like a dog kennel. I try to brush my teeth twice a day and I also brush my tongue, even though that often triggers my gag reflex, making me sick and therefore twice as smelly as when I started.

MUSKY SAUSAGE

POUR BEAR

Spring in My Step

The warm air fills me up with joy
The birds tweet in the sky
Today I think I'll fall in love
I don't really know why

But as the hours tick on by
I still feel quite alone
I hear a bird laugh at me
So I pick up a stone

I try to hit the bird but miss
And suddenly I jolt
To see the stone strike a car
Which screeches to a halt

The police step out so I run off
I fall and hurt my knee
Forcing me to spend the night
Hiding up a tree

—○—

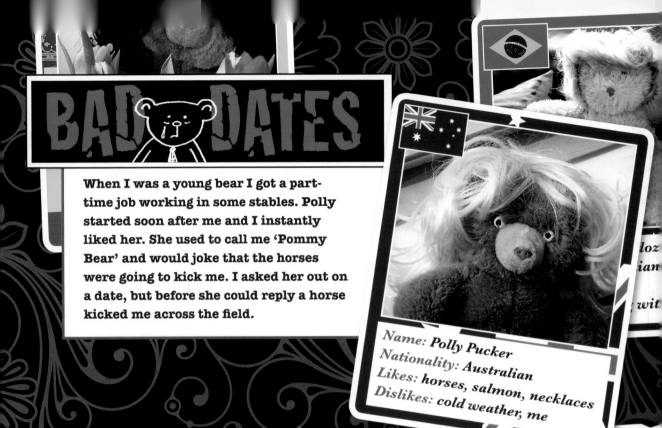

BAD DATES

When I was a young bear I got a part-time job working in some stables. Polly started soon after me and I instantly liked her. She used to call me 'Pommy Bear' and would joke that the horses were going to kick me. I asked her out on a date, but before she could reply a horse kicked me across the field.

Name: **Polly Pucker**
Nationality: **Australian**
Likes: **horses, salmon, necklaces**
Dislikes: **cold weather, me**

My Diary — Monday

9am: Ants have got in the food cupboard. Can't remember how to get rid of ants. Do you pour salt on them?

11am: Have to throw out all my food - ants are even in my ice cream! Feel hungry so go to the shops.

1pm: Get back from the shops and realise I forgot to get salt to put on the ants. Decide to use sugar instead.

3pm: Shouldn't have put sugar on the ants as my kitchen is now full of ants. Apparently ants LIKE sugar.

5pm: Find seven ants in my bed. Not a good day.

MiseryBear

My horoscope today just said 'You will have a rubbish day. Don't get out of bed.' I might take them up on that.

about 5 hours ago via Twitbear for iPaw

@MiseryBear: I was just sick on myself. I guess I shouldn't have had all that Baileys and pizza before bed. Blurgh.
15th March

@MiseryBear: I crushed two sleeping pills into my pasta and now my paws feel all fuzzy.
10th March

@MiseryBear: It's Friday night, I'm eating a microwave meal for one, and I think my neighbours are having sex. Kill me.
4th March

@MiseryBear: I got stuck in my recycling bin the other day. It made my fur smell.
25th Feb

@MiseryBear: Screw you, @ratbanjos. You're a stinky mean human and if I get the chance I'll bite you.
10th Feb

@ratbanjos: Hey, @MiseryBear. Why don't you stop moaning and grow a pair?
10th Feb

@MiseryBear: I just coughed up a furball on the train. How embarrassing!
29th Jan

@MiseryBear: Ohh wowserbs! i'ms a drunnk bear right now? HEllo! whoo you lookin aT? I <3 you! xxOOx
3rd Jan

@MiseryBear: I'd like to say this was the worst Christmas ever, but last year I caught my fur on a candle and had to go to A&E. Actually, this was worse.
25th Dec

Name Misery Bear
Location Hell, Earth
Web www.misery...
Bio I'm drunk, angry, depressed, lonely, sad, drunk, annoyed, fluffy and drunk. What about you?

885   following

9   followers

1   listed

Winks   **2,436**

Favourites

following

view all...

Romantic Recipes

I've always liked cooking for other people, and even if they don't fall in love with you, at least they'll usually help with the washing up.

FISH & EGGS

In the wild, bears eat live salmon and raw eggs out of bird nests. I personally think this is gross, but serving up a poached fillet of salmon with a sunny side up fried egg is very fancy. Although my eggs always come out chewy.

PIZZA

I love pizzas. The best pizza I ever made contained ham, rocket, capers, ice cream, apple, tuna, beef, honey, gorgonzola and strawberries. Although the girl I cooked it for is now dead.

STEAK & CHIPS

Gnashing on a giant slab of rare meat whilst gazing into your lover's eyes is very romantic, unless you get a bit of gristle stuck between your teeth and have to yank it out with your paws (not a hot look). In films, tough guys eat steaks but it really plays havoc with my IBS.

How To Serve a Romantic Meal

- 🐾 Dim the lights
- 🐾 Serve the first course
- 🐾 Apologise for spilling hot soup on date
- 🐾 Put lights back on quickly
- 🐾 Phone ambulance
- 🐾 Ask date if she fancies coming over when she's out of burns ward

Dear Pamela

i went to the ThiRsty Frog and waited for you but you didn't arrive. i hope everything is OK? Today i went for a wALk and walked so far i enDeD up at the sea. i had to stop waLking othERwise I would have drowned!

Pamela, i can't stop thinking about you. i think i'm in loaf with you. Sorry, that was a mistake. i meant love. i am a very nice bear And i thInk you would like me. i am clever and kind and i don't lose my tumper.. i HATE THiS TYPE WRiTERRRRRRRrR woUld you like to come over for dinner? i can maKE lots of things but mainly pasta. i can make soMmething for your dog, too. Does he like pasta?

misery bear xx

BAD DATES

One day I did a sponsored bounce on a spacehopper for Comic Relief. No one would sponsor me though, and I was just about to give up when I knocked on one last door. It turned out to be Kate Moss's house. She invited me in and we got pretty drunk together. Then she whispered in my ear that she had 'something special' to show me upstairs. I thought we were going to make love, but it turned out she had a shrine to me. Bit bonkers, tbh. I got out of there fast, but she chased me down the road and I got hit by a car. When I woke up, she had me locked in her spare room. We ended up an item (after she hobbled me) and dated for a couple of years. It was fun, but I got a bit tired of all the paparazzis. I broke it off and she sent me some VERY angry texts. The last one just said, 'YOU'RE MINE, BEAR!' Brrrrr.

Name: **Kate Moss**
Occupation: **model**
Likes: **fashion, music, parties**
Dislikes: **restraining orders**

do's and don'ts of Meeting the Parents

Do: compliment the mother on her clothes
Don't: compliment the father on his clothes

Do: mention where you first met
Don't: mention your first hump

Do: tell them your ambitions
Don't: promise to achieve them

Do: bring a bottle a booze as a gift
Don't: drink it all yourself

top 5 movies to weep into a hanky to

There's nothing better than having a good cry at the pictures, it really clears out your tear ducts. These are the top 5 films that make my eyes do a salty wee...

★CINEMA★
ADMIT ONE
LOSER

Field of Dreams
I have dad issues. Very few bears don't. So when Kevin Costner's baseball ghost dad appears and... sniff... asks to play catch with him I... sniff... I can't go on....

Beaches
When I was a little bear I sneaked into the cinema to see this because I thought it would be a nice film about holidays and sunshine and such. It wasn't. It was about a lady dying... sniff.

The Perfect Storm
It's sad cos a) it's true and, b) a load of nice fishermen drowning on a boat is sad, end of story. Oh, is that a spoiler? Sorry.

Old Yeller
Faithful dog defends family, ends up getting shot. When I first saw this I had to pretend there was chili powder in my eye. I'm not sure my date was convinced (never saw her again).

It's A Wonderful Life
See? I'm not the most miserable bear in the world. I cry at happy endings too. I watch this film every Christmas, on my own, with a bottle of sherry. And I sob my little furry heart out.

MY FIRST LOVE

BAD DATES

I met Gina at a gym and she made me dizzy with love. At least I think that's why I was dizzy – I had just fallen off a running machine. Gina had beautiful blue eyes and dark hair like a black cat. She smiled at me and I thought that meant she was in love with me too. She agreed to go on a date, but she stood me up. I never saw her again, but in my dreams we are married and she loves me more than anybody in the entire world.

Name: *Gina Sparkles*
Nationality: *Spanish*
Likes: *everything*
Dislikes: *nothing, me*

My Diary — Wednesday

7am: Woken up by a crow flying in through my window and landing on my bed. It tried to peck my ears then flew out.

8am: Cold shower. Not through choice, but because of a burst main down the road. Can't wash soap out of my fur.

9:07am: Late for work by seven minutes. Boss shouts at me in front of whole office. What a dick.

2pm: I sneak out of work and go for a walk.

4pm: Fall asleep under a tree in the park. Wake up to find a crow looking at me. Is it the same one?

1am: Wake up in middle of night – crow nightmares!

misery bear's
HOMEMADE COCKTAILS

MOUNTIE'S MILKSHAKE

I was introduced to this drink by a bartender in Canada. He told me he was a real hit with the ladies and that if I drank enough of these I would be too. So I drank fifteen of them. Maybe it was the maple syrup that made me so sick, maybe it was the whisky. Either way, the only lady I got talking to was the nurse who pumped my tummy.

— a miserable life —

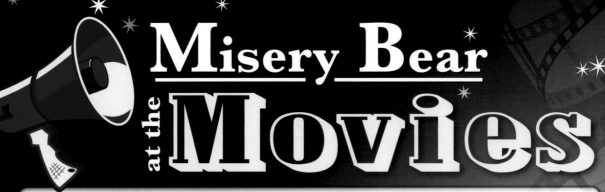

Misery Bear at the Movies

For some reason, the people who run the BBC Comedy website like making little documentary films about my awful life. It's actually quite humiliating, but they pay me in whisky so I go along with it. Here are a few of them...

MISERY BEAR GOES TO WORK

This film was my idea – I wanted to show people the crushing boredom of my stupid job, and how I got fired from it. Everything that happens in it is true – my nodding bird buddy, the measly cheese slice in my sandwich, my asshole boss... utter hell.

MISERY BEAR GOES TO THE SEASIDE

I went to the beach in Brighton to get over my break-up with Daisy Barkington, the love of my life. Well, she was the love of MY life. She told me afterwards she never loved me, and often couldn't remember my name. I was sick on the rollercoaster, a seagull crapped on my chips and my photo of me and Daisy got washed away by the sea. And yes, I fell in too.

MISERY BEAR'S VALENTINE'S DAY

I've never actually received a valentine, so when I went out to buy replacement booze after realising I was going to be spending the day on my own, as usual, I caught the eye of a pretty girl in the window of my local (The Bridge House in Penge). I thought she wanted me. I rushed to buy her flowers and chocolates, it was love at first sight. But no, she was waiting for her boyfriend, a speccy berk. Sigh.

MISERY BEAR PREPARES FOR A DATE

I'd met a nice lady in a bar and she agreed to come over for dinner. I couldn't believe my luck so I spent the day grooming myself and cooking a fancy meal. Well, it looked fancy in the book, but it looked like cat sick when I served it up. Needn't have bothered though – she never showed up. Another night on my own watching Channel 5 with a six pack of lager.

Misery Bear's Late Night Thoughts

Double whisky please

I should have showered

wrestling

Is there a God for bears?

I want to be a baby bear again

Explosions

Imagine being a wasp!

Jessica Alba

Why does no one hug me?

Why am I alive?

BAD DATES

I got really drunk with Belinda years ago for three days. I don't remember where it was but at one point she said we were in Vegas, although I have no memory of this. I do remember that she was crazy, swore lots, and kept saying I was a 'dead bear' if I ever left her. She kept wanting to tie me up, which I thought was weird, so I jumped on a train when she wasn't looking. It reminded me that love is crazy – because she was completely insane.

Name: Belinda Knash
Nationality: American
Likes: sambuca

rkles
nish
ng
ng, me

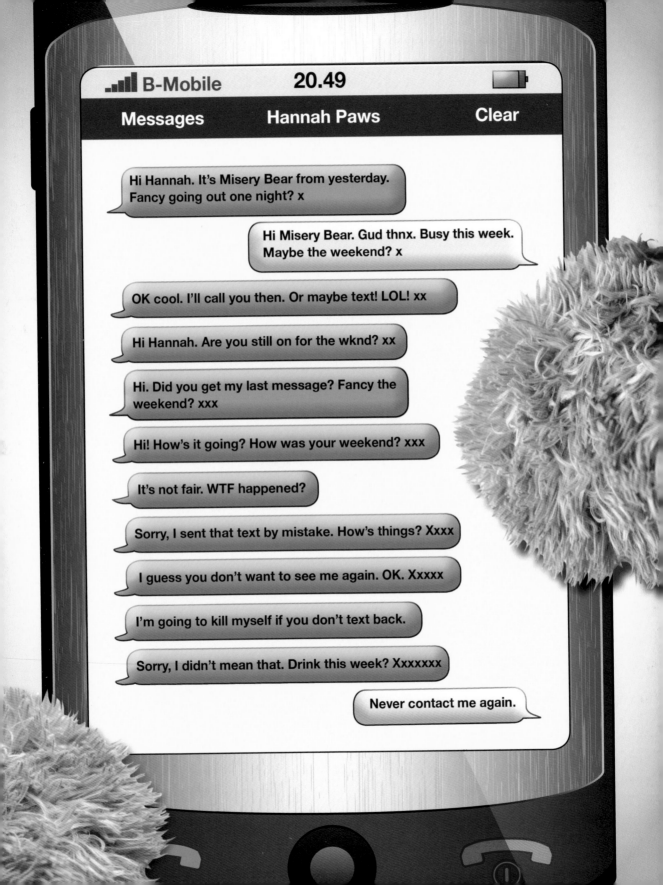

how to.. End a Relationship

So let's say you've met me, I mean somebody, but you don't want to see him or her any more. How do you end it? Here are some options for you heartbreakers out there.*

FACE-TO-FACE FAILURE

If you're no longer interested in me (I mean a person), invite them out for an evening. Buy them dinner and chat like everything is fine. Then, toward the end of the night, break the news that it's all over. Watch my face – I mean the person's face – as the despair sinks in. Then order cheesecake.

JILTED BY PHONE

The phone rings. I... I mean YOU answer, and it's your sweetheart telling you she doesn't want to be your sweetheart any more. Your eyes start to wee-wee. Whenever this happens to me I try to make the conversation last as long as possible so I'm at least running up their phone bill.

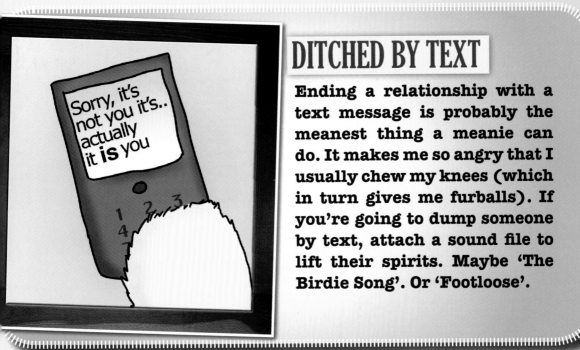

DITCHED BY TEXT

Ending a relationship with a text message is probably the meanest thing a meanie can do. It makes me so angry that I usually chew my knees (which in turn gives me furballs). If you're going to dump someone by text, attach a sound file to lift their spirits. Maybe 'The Birdie Song'. Or 'Footloose'.

SIMPLY VANISH

OK, so you met me – I mean a person – in a bar. You laughed, talked, and even exchanged numbers. But now you've changed your mind, and for some reason meeting up with me – I mean, that person – no longer appeals. So you don't answer calls, texts or emails, but just vanish like it never happened. This leaves me – I mean, the person – feeling confused and empty. And when that happens I eat A LOT of pizza. Stupid fat bear.

* This is not in any way based on personal experience. **
** It is.

Love Letter #3

Dear Pamela

i hOPe you got mY last letter. and thE
nine i sEnt before thAt. i won't write
again. ALso, my tYpewrittter is running
out of ink, so i can't wRite any moOre
leTters anyw4y.

RiGht now, i'm going to have a little
drink and think aBout you. i'll have one
drink for evRry time i think oF you. you
will alWays have a place in my heart,
pAmela...

m sery bear...

misery bear's
HOMEMADE COCKTAILS

I've never understood why people put olives in a martini. There's a time and a place for everything, but please don't put any olives in my drinks. In my version, I've substituted the olive for a chocolate, which is much better. I've also substituted the vermouth, which I think tastes gross. Basically, it's a strawberry milkshake with gin in it. Delicious.

MISERY martini

— a miserable life —

My Diary — Friday

10am Run to get the train. Very late!

10.05 Realise I've forgotten my money. Run back home to get it.

10.10 Run to get the train.

10.15 Get to the train station too late. Throw a doughnut at a train.

10.16 Get chased out of the train station.

10.20 Trip over a dog. Get chased home.

top 5 tearjerky books that make me cry

I'm a well-educated bear and I read a lot of literature. And the sadder the book, the more it speaks to my tiny soul...

5 **Marley & Me by John Grogan**
Anything sad with dogs in it will get me boo-hooing, although most mutts don't actually like me. Marley would have probably torn me apart.

4 **Of Mice and Men by John Steinbeck**
If you can read the final pages of this book without crying then I don't know you (although it really helps to read all the other pages first).

3 **The Bell Jar by Sylvia Plath**
She killed herself shortly after writing it. I'm just hoping THIS book doesn't have me following in Sylvia's footsteps.

2 **One Flew Over the Cuckoo's Nest by Ken Kesey**
I did a spell in rehab a few years back but it was nothing like this. One of the nurses was a bit like Nurse Ratchett. She confiscated my hip flask.

1 **Atonement by Ian McEwan**
I won't spoil it, but the revelation in this hits harder than anything in any book ever. It's bigger than 'I'm your father, Luke' and a lot sadder.

BEAR WITH THE WIND

SCENE 118

INT. POSH MANSION. DAY

MISERY BEAR is walking down a staircase. SCARLET O' BEARA is
running after him, crying.

> SCARLET
> Misery! Why are you going away?

> MISERY
> I've had enough of it here. There's
> nothing to do and I need to do some
> washing.

> SCARLET
> I want to come with you!

> MISERY
> You can't. Besides, my place isn't
> big enough for all your shoes.

MISERY BEAR walks down to the door and SCARLET runs after
him. She really likes him because he's the best bear she's
ever met.

> SCARLET
> But what shall I do with myself?

MISERY BEAR turns to her and puts on his hat.

what type of hat??

> MISERY
> Frankly my bear, I don't give a damn.

MISERY BEAR walks out of the house.

> SCARLET
> But Misery Bear - I love you!
> Please marry me!

she should kiss me loads here

MISERY BEAR stops and looks at her.

> MISERY
> Oh. Really? Oh ok. Come on then.

They go and live happily ever after and MISERY BEAR is never
sad again.

i've just realised the title of this makes it sound like i hare the farts... OH GOD!!

note: make sure the actress likes bears

Sunset of Our Love

You used to mean the world to me
I thought you were the one
But then you left with someone else
I blinked and you were gone

If the ending could be different
We'd still be having fun
Riding off on a horse
Into the setting sun

Our love is just a memory now
Of images and sounds
And now I wish I'd never lent you
Three thousand pounds

——○——

So there you have it. That was my guide to love, but mainly heartbreak. I hope you learned something, dear reader. I know I have. I've learned that writing a book really hurts my paws.

So if you ever see a sad, lonely, and possibly drunk bear wandering the streets, spare a thought for him. He's probably me. Give him a wave, a smile, and maybe even a kiss if you're a pretty lady. Because one day, surely, this heartache will end...

misery bear
xx

ACKNOWLEDGEMENTS

Misery Bear was assisted by
Chris Hayward & Nat Saunders

Book Design by
Pete Shirley

With thanks to:

Jon Petrie, Ash Atalla, Tim Sealey, Bertie Peek, Paul Doolan, Becky Murrell, Ed Petrie,
Olly Cambridge, Holly Walsh, Susy Kane, Kate Moss, Martin Trickey, Will Saunders, Matt Stronge,
Suszi Saunders, Camille Aznar, Janette Linden, Mary McCallum, Kirsty Shirley, Lisa Highton,
Valerie Appleby, Lucy Zilberkweit, the Hayward Family, the Saunders Family
and everyone who has supported Misery Bear through his darkest times

'The Bear Who Loved Me' and 'Bear With The Wind' illustrations by
Leighton Johns

'Celebrity Love List' images (page 13) courtesy of:
Cinemafestival/Shutterstock (top left), Entertainment Press/Shutterstock (right),
Dfree/Shutterstock (bottom)

First published in Great Britain in 2011 by Hodder & Stoughton
An Hachette UK company

A CIP catalogue record for this title is available from the British Library

Hardback ISBN 978 1 444 72805 7

Printed and bound in Spain by Cayfosa Impresia Iberica S. A.

Hodder & Stoughton policy is to use papers that are natural, renewable and recyclable products and
made from wood grown in sustainable forests. The logging and manufacturing processes are expected
to conform to the environmental regulations of the country of origin.

Hodder & Stoughton Ltd
338 Euston Road
London NW1 3BH

www.hodder.co.uk